Praise for the Author

In *The Gifts of Dyslexia*, **Mike DeLong** takes you on his personal journey of dealing with, as Mike puts it, a **DiFForder** or a **DiFFability**. Through his journey, Mike not only helps you understand what dyslexia is, but gives you a proven process that has given him and those who have worked with him the awareness that dyslcxia in many ways has been a gift. I highly recommend *The Gifts of Dyslexia* for those with the diagnosis and also caregivers, teachers, and family members wanting to help and support.

Gary Barnes President
GaryBarnesInternational.com

Most people are so concerned with the stigma of being diagnosed with dyslexia that they miss the gifts that come along with it. Mike has a passion and wisdom for teaching the tools he has used himself through the years to become a successful business person, trainer, and coach. This is a great book to share with anyone who wants to make a DIFFerence in the life of someone who has The Gift of Dyslexia.

Tonja Waring
Founder, The Manifesting Mindset

Gratitude

To the many individuals I have met in my life, there is no such thing as a self-made man.

It takes the courage of others to step into your life and accept you as you are. To unconditionally walk with you, talk with you, accept the flaws as they are, and inspire you to a greater good. To be a true friend.

I also want to specifically acknowledge:

Ron Jackson, Ph.D. For taking the time to edit this book, for writing the introduction, your praise for the author. For a lifetime of mentorship and friendship.

Pastor Bill Farr. We met in the early 70's and I was mesmerized by your courage and faith in God. That has never wavered in all these years. To lead by example is many times easier said than done. To this day you still do it. An example I cherish and follow.

Gary Barnes. For your kindness and forgiveness. For your mentorship and inspiration. For reviving that little genius within me and for inspiring me to take on a Goliath in my life.

Tonja Waring. For your kindness and forgiveness. For sharing your story. We all think we have the worst or hardest things to deal with until we hear someone else's story.

Dedicated to

My daughter, Jackie. A powerful woman who does nothing but help others. Her determination and unwavering strength are her gift to others.

My son, Troy. Though his life was short the lives he touched were many. His happy-go-lucky nature and his half-moon smile were his gift to others.

May 26, 1980 – September 12, 2007

And, the many individuals who knowingly or unknowingly struggle with Dyslexia.

The Gifts of Dyslexia

by Mike DeLong

CONTENTS

The Gifts of Dyslexia

Foreword

GARY BARNES

It's very special when you find an individual who is willing to not only identify a challenge and then share their own personal struggle with the challenge but also to take up the mission to address the challenge head-on to help others.

Mike Delong has done just that in his book *The Gifts of Dyslexia*. You might ask, "Why does Mike say that being a dyslexic is a gift?" Good question. Because it is! Dyslexia is not a disability but a difference, as Mike refers to it as simply a Difforder and a Diffability.

Because there are no apparent signs, dyslexia is invisible so it can be misunderstood by the outside world. That's why this book is so valuable, because Mike takes you on his personal journey. Finding out what I call *workarounds* is what Mike did in school, the military and as a business owner. He wasn't willing to accept a label of being slow or somehow less capable of accomplishing what he wanted to in life than any other person.

Mike also has a passion for anyone who is dealing with dyslexia, their teachers, parents and partners to provide them with the dynamics and science about what they deal with on a daily basis. By no means are they deficient or broken. They are just different and by understanding what is happening physically, they then have permission to embrace that difference as a gift.

Mike is not satisfied with just telling his story and giving the reader an understanding of dyslexia. Mike takes it to a whole new level by providing tools and processes that allow the reader to develop their own personal system to achieve their own level of success in their lives.

As someone who has worked with Mike and now considers him a friend, I can tell you that he is one of the most genuine, deep-thinking, and giving human beings on the planet.

This may sound strange, but please do not just read this book. My encouragement to you is to study this book to get the full value and impact that Mike has put into these pages. Then reach out to Mike and his community to connect with individuals who will give you support and understanding.

One of my Garyisms is "Life is a solo journey, traveled with many." You don't have to take this journey alone. Learn from those who have gone before you, embrace those who will walk beside you, and lead those who will follow in your footsteps.

Welcome to your first day of your magnificence!

Gary Barnes
President, Gary Barnes International
International Speaker, Author and Business Coach
www.GaryBarnesInternational.com

Introduction

RON JACKSON, PH.D.

Dyslexia is the most common learning disability in the form of reading, writing, and spelling difficulties. It has been nearly 140 years since **Oswald Berkhan** was the first to describe the disorder. Berkhan was a German physician who championed special education and care for the mentally ill and disadvantaged learners. He advocated for research into this ailment. A few years later, the German Ophthalmologist, **Rudolf Berlin**, actually coined the term *dyslexia* (derived from two Greek words, "dys" and "lexis" essentially meaning "difficulty with words or speech").

Estimates range between 5 to 12 percent of school-aged children are affected by dyslexia. The percentage of all people who have dyslexia may be as high as 17%. It is extremely important to recognize, diagnose, and provide guidance and proper educational aides for this ailment early in a child's life. If left neglected or overlooked, the dyslexic individual will be on a course faced with certain hardships, possible embarrassment, and recurrent misunderstandings. While all the underlying influences and pathologies of this disorder are not fully discovered or known at this writing, there is much that has been uncovered with the environmental, genetic, and anatomical factors associated with this malady.

In this book, the author, Mike Delong, provides in-depth clinical and personal reflections on this so-called disorder. Mike, who is a dyslexic, offers readers principally those parents who have dyslexic children, insight into how dyslexia is a gift, not a burden or negative. The reader who is especially dyslexic or for those who care for or know an affected individual will immediately relate to Mike's accounting of his personal journey; his experiences in early schooling, transformation into adulthood, and how he adapted his "malady" into a unique tool for managing his life's encounters. Mike also delves into the current scientific and anatomical facts underlying the behavioral characteristics of dyslexia. The reader should be able to come away with a better appreciation and understanding of how the dyslexic brain perceives and processes visual, audible, and non-audible input, especially in language regions of the brain. Without an understanding of why and how the dyslexic brain works, data input can lead to chaos and frustration. Once one grasps the problems and challenges facing the dyslexic mind, where, unlike a non-dyslexic brain, perceived information has to jump from the right to the left brain hemispheres, the dyslexic individual may learn to harness the power of this unique condition. This is well demonstrated by the many successful individuals such as the great inventor, Thomas Edison, the titan of industry, Henry Ford, the mind behind the iPhone, Steve Jobs, the movie mogul, Steven Spielberg, the premier comedian, Robin Williams, Microsoft founder, Bill Gates to name just a small portion of dyslexics.

Ron Jackson, Ph.D.
Friend and Colleague

A Word from the Author

MIKE DELONG

I write this book as a testimony of how the life of a dyslexic might unfold. It is not a boast of accomplishments but, a reflection of events that transpired in my life which I could not explain until I understood dyslexia and being Left-Handed.

As many dyslexics I have encountered along the way will tell you, their success was not in spite of dyslexia, but because of it.

As science gains on what the causes and effects of Dyslexia are, what I call being a Right-Brainer, the Gifts of Dyslexia start to emerge.

You can't cure Dyslexia because it's not a disease.
Dyslexics aren't broken so you can't fix them. Their
Brains are just different. ~ Ben Foss

I do not have a Disorder or a Disability.
I have a DiFForder and a DiFFability.
My DiFForder is: I process information
differently than others.
My DiFFability is, I access areas of my
brain that others may not. ~ Mike DeLong

Do not discount the power of dyslexics. Without dyslexics from the past and present like Thomas Edison, Henry Ford, Benjamin Franklin, Bill Gates, Steve Jobs, William Hullett (HP), Walt Disney, or Steven Spielberg, the world might not have Lights, Cars, Phones or Cell Phones, Computers or good movies to watch. These are just a few dyslexics that have succeeded because of their dyslexia.

CHAPTER 1

Genesis

In the beginning, my father begat my mother and that is how they begot me. Yes, from the start, they should have known I would be energetic seeing as how my mother had a bruise the size of a basketball on her belly.

CHAPTER 2

Watch Out for This Kid

My mother said I was born walking. My father said I never walked a day in my life, I just ran! At the age of seven months, I figured out what my legs would do for me, and I was on the go. Along with the early physical development, I was also one of those kids who had a very vivid imagination.

From the time we are born, we pretty much live life and are directed from our right brain. When we begin formal schooling, we are forced into using our left brain such as our language skills which are contained in lobes on the left side of our brain.

Another early life-conflict was that my mother wanted me to be right-handed. In those days, there was still a negative stigma about being left-handed. Consequently, my mother would make me sit on my left hand during meals to force me to switch hands. I would joke with my mother by telling her that sitting on my left hand would not stop me from eating. It didn't. Finally, one day my father said to leave him alone, he's going to be what he is going to be. A very prophetic statement.

I took my first ride in a police car at the age of three. Being an Acutely Aware individual, I noticed that when we were going to the store, my mother would get dressed, throw her purse over her shoulder, grab my hand, and off we would go for the six-block walk to the store. So, I decided one day I was going to try this on my own. I threw my mother's purse over my shoulder, just like she did, and off I went. Well, I got about five blocks into my journey and came to the intersection where we normally would cross using the stop light. As I stood on the curb contemplating how I was going to accomplish crossing this massive street, people started to gather around and began asking me questions, like "Where do you live?"

"I don't know."

As luck would have it I grabbed my mother's purse, but I didn't check to see if her wallet was inside. Oops! Hey, what's a wallet? I'm three! So they called the police. Into the back of the police car, I went. No handcuffs of course because they are way too big for a three-year-old!

I'm in the back seat, on my knees, looking out the side back window thinking, *WOW, this is cool!* The police officer asked me "Do you know where you live?"

I said, "No, but there's my dad!" Now, seeing the look on my dad's face and after living with him for a whole three years, I knew at this very moment that I was better off with the police.

CHAPTER 3

Something is Wrong with This Kid

It was in my early grade school years that my parents and teachers discovered something wasn't quite right with me. They wondered for an active kid like me, *why did I come home from school and go to bed?* Well, I told my parents that by the time I got done with school, I'd have these massive headaches. Two things were behind the problems. One, I needed glasses! The second, they never figured out. I always had trouble reading, especially out loud. I would spend a ridiculous number of hours trying to write a book report. A statement that was aimed at me by many of my teachers that I will never forget as long as I live, was "Quit your dreaming and pay attention!"

Hum, I thought I was!

Through the administrative interventions to my so-called lack of learning and focus, I was forced in having to take all kinds of special classes because I had a learning disability. One of these special classes that I remember the most was during an entire summer where I had to sit in a very hot classroom. The teacher would flash up on the wall in green light, a word, and I had to read the word.

Did it help? Not to my knowledge.

After that summer class of torture, I didn't feel that I could read any better or any worse. For most of my schooling years, the academic side of it was HELL. I did, however, make it through high school graduating in the middle of my class. That was just fine with me as a lot of my friends never got that far.

CHAPTER 4

The Instigator

As a very young child, my mother called me an *instigator*. Hum… Is that a synonym for a leader? She said I was always starting something. Now, I wasn't sure if it was a good or bad thing. But according to my parents (friends, teachers?), I was known for starting trouble. However, many times I was starting good things. Such as in the neighborhood, I would start a baseball team, or I would put together a game of 500 because no one else would. If you want to play baseball, somebody has got to put together the team. This ensures there is a team and you're on it. This continued up to high school and I guess for that matter throughout the rest of my life. So, I guess I could be called an instigator.

You know we all have these moments in life where something somebody says or something somebody does either inspires us or sets us back in life. One of those moments for me was in the fifth grade and was centered on athletics.

I'm sure you probably remember the field day at your school. This is the day where they have several events and you compete against your classmates. This day was a special day for me being an athlete which was something I excelled at.

On this day we had five events scheduled. I was able to win all five events. Now, that would seem to be a very high moment for most kids and it was for me, however, returning to class my teacher stopped me and said, "I see you have five blue ribbons and one of them is for running. You will probably be running from the police the rest of your life."

I remembered what an impact it had when he said that. Why would somebody say that, and squash a major accomplishment in that kind of way? I suppose there was a good reason for his statement. As my life unfolded, those who knew me stated that they expected to see me behind bars. But then, they told many other kids the same thing.

As I advanced through high school, athletics was my strong suit. I was not the kind of person that excelled in academics (for good reason). I wasn't horrible at school, some A's, B's a lot of C's but I always felt more comfortable in an athletic environment. In fact, athletics got me through school. If it had not been for sports eligibility, I'm sure that I would have failed more classes than I did. Being eligible for sports was a major thing in my life. For instance, I remember my junior high counselor telling me that if I stuck to the curriculum and just the required curriculum for high school, I could finish high school and graduate in the 11th grade. Well, I took that to heart and completed high school at the end of the 11th grade.

To be eligible for sports in my senior year, I had to take at least two classes. Therefore, I took gym and gymnastics. My school day went like this: I took an automotive course during the morning half of the day. Then I went to high school in the afternoon. The great thing about this schedule is that I would go to my gymnastics class after which I headed to my gym class and then to the fields for practice. I had been groomed for pro baseball in my high school years, and I expected to go play for a minor league team (The Denver Bears) upon graduating from high school. I thought I was set as far as a career went and I actually did get drafted by the largest team in the world, The United States Armed Forces!

CHAPTER 5

Drafted

At the time I was pretty devastated knowing that I had just lost a baseball career. In retrospect, it was probably the best thing that ever happened to me.

When I reported to the Induction Center, for some reason the military didn't want to hear about my baseball career. There was a war going on, and I was going - that's all there was to it. Concerning that matter, I'd like to say now that I am an educated man as opposed to an arrogant baseball player.

When I think back on all the twists and turns my military career path took me, I know now that it was God's plan and not my plan. The important qualities that the military taught me about myself and leadership, I am certain, I would not have gotten very far in the civilian world.

As I was leaving on the trip to basic training, I remember struggling with what I had just lost; maybe having a successful baseball career and all it would have brought, but now I was left trying to accept the severe intimidation and adversity that I was about to incur in basic training. I made up my mind though, that no matter what the military training did, I was not going to let them get to me. They are looking for a "Breaking Point" and as far as I was concerned, I didn't have one.

Being in excellent athletic condition paid off very well in basic training. However, some strange things started to happen that I didn't exactly understand at the time. About a week into Air Force basic training, the training instructor came up and asked me if I could be a Guide-on. This is the individual who marches in front of the flight (troop formation) and carries the squadron flag. I was a little baffled by the question since we already had one, I didn't know why he was asking me. But, I said of course, and at that point, I became the flight's new Guide-on. A little further into basic training, I was asked to be a Flight Leader. This is an individual who is excelling in training and is expected to lead and help others through their training. This also meant that that anytime there was going to be a flight inspection I would do a pre-inspection to assist other individuals with their lockers and beds to help reduce the number of demerits.

Now it's time to graduate and receive our assignments. Now we are all wondering what we are going to become in the Air Force and where we would be going to do that job, I am pulled aside and our Training Instructor asked if I would like to be a Training Instructor for the Air Force. I graciously declined and said I was looking to see the world that's why I was in the Air Force.

The next day we graduated, and I received my assignment as a Weapons Technician. I remember thinking, *what the heck is that?* It was disappointing to think that I might be cleaning M16 rifles for the next four years. As it turned out, I would be working on the Weapons Systems of various fighter aircraft, much different than I expected.

CHAPTER 6

Next Stop: Tech School, Lowry Air Force Base, Colorado.

On my first day arriving at tech school, I was again pulled aside by one of the instructors and asked if I could be a class leader. I thought to myself; I don't see why not. What does a class leader do? In hindsight, I should have asked that question in reverse and had him explain what a class leader does. But, he said as a class leader I would march the class to various appointments, to various classes, to the chow hall, and give out various assignments. It still didn't seem to be that big a deal. So I accepted and became the class leader.

At this point, I'm starting to wonder why I am continually being singled out for these types of assignments. There must be a sign on my forehead that I can't see saying, "Give it to Mikey he'll do it".

I graduated from Tech School as an Honor Student which allowed me to pick my base of choice for my first assignment. That became Mountain Home Air Force Base in Idaho. I would be working on the newest fighter aircraft in the Air Force inventory which was the F-111 models.

Now, I am enjoying some of my life's new freedoms and disciplines and I am beginning a career in weapons release systems on the F-111. This is what I was made for; I was learning a new trade, and I wanted to excel. I became the chief troubleshooter of the F-111-F models. That meant when the aircraft deployed for special assignments such as Red Flag, which is the equivalent of the Navy Top Gun, I was the individual who went with the aircraft for those exercises.

CHAPTER 7

Next Stop: Germany

This assignment came about in a very strange way. When entering the Air Force, you get to put in what is called a Dream Sheet. This is a way of letting the Air Force know what assignment areas you might like to go to such as Thailand or Europe or just remain in the US. Well, when I entered the Air Force, my Dream Sheet destination from the beginning was Europe. After two years at Mountain Home Idaho, I wanted to go somewhere else and "see the world" as they say.

Then it finally happened; I got an assignment. It's in Bitburg, Germany. Hold on! There's a catch. Just two days later, I am assigned to Thailand. Now talk about being confused. There is no clarity as to which one I have to go to. So, I called MPC (Man Power Center) and asked, which one do I have to go to? Now, I'm sure you're probably aware that the military never asks you anything. It is always for the "good of the Air Force". However, when I got MPC on the line, and told them that I had two assignments and asked, "which assignment do I have to go to". Their reply was, "Which one do you want to go to?"

Now, I am a little stunned and thinking, are you kidding me? I, of course, said, "Germany!"

The reply came back, "Okay then! Go to Germany".

My assignment in Germany was not overly eventful but with one exception. About a year into it, I was asked if I would be a training instructor for my career field. Because my four-year commitment was almost over and Vietnam was winding down, I had set my focus on getting out of the military. As you might guess, I was not overly excited about being a weapons technician or teaching others to be a weapons technician.

There was one event that happened at this time that was very exciting to me. I got to play in a Semi-Pro Football League. Yes, there was good old American football in Europe and the military fielded teams to play other military teams in Europe. I played Linebacker. That position suited me very well as I had the size combined with the speed to become a devastating force on the field. I was so proficient at linebacker that I was selected to be a defensive captain. Eventually, I was also selected to be a team captain. Very special times for me!

Another area I found very exciting was skiing. During my high school years, I was a skier and loved it. All my ski buddies would tell me that someday they were going to ski in Europe. My reply? Yeah right! Well, I was the lucky one. I was able to ski in seven different countries and was able to attend the 1976 Winter Olympics in Innsbruck, Austria.

Yes, the Colorado kid, the supposed trouble-maker, did well!

Finally, I separated after my four-year military commitment was up and returned to the civilian world. My focus changed leading me to spend the next six years working a variety of jobs and raising a family.

CHAPTER 8

Something Very Special

In my first four years of military service, I met a lot of guys; some who were well-educated and some with very little education. When meeting new individuals, you usually start by comparing notes or life experiences. To my astonishment, I found a lot of guys who struggled in school the same way I did. Many had been lumped into the same category as myself (a learning disability or a slow learner), but some had been diagnosed with Dyslexia. As I heard more and more about this Dyslexia, it fit! I'm thinking "Ah ha!" There is a name for this beast that has plagued me for years.

I never placed much weight or thought into dyslexia being the underlying problem because after graduating high school and interacting with others, it didn't seem to me that I had any hang-ups. I attribute that to my athletic training and mindset that is; work with what you have and give your best. And because of my physical abilities, others considered me to be a leader; certainly, didn't see me a weak or lacking intellect.

Thinking back on my life, the other thing that left a big impression on me as a child was the fact that I was always in the midst of physically challenged children. My older sister had a neuro-muscular condition similar to Muscular Dystrophy (MD), and two other MD children were growing up on the same block. This steered our family into spending a lot of time in events associated with MD children. These individuals never saw themselves as physically or mentally challenged. Their attitude was always positive, and forward-thinking, more like a "what can I do and how can I accomplish it?"

If you don't want an affliction to affect you, it is better you don't know what it is.

In comparison to these children, "I ain't got nut'n'!" But having experienced this relationship with these individuals helped to mold my attitude to life's challenges.

CHAPTER 9

Back in
(Very Strange)

After being out of the military for six years, I happened to have a casual conversation with a recruiter one day. It was just a general conversation, but he easily determined that I was prior military. When he found out that I was a Weapons Tech, his face kind of perked up. He inquired whether I knew that in my career field, the Air Force would give me all my rank back and a $20,000 bonus to reenter the military. My first reaction was shock. Then being the wise veteran that I am, I ask him to show me where the regulations state that. He pulls out a manual and sure enough, that is exactly what it says, with one catch. I missed the 20,000 dollar bonus by 30 days. Well, the main thing I was looking for was the rank. The rank is also your pay grade. If I couldn't get my rank back, I didn't feel I could support a family of four.

Well as you probably guessed, I returned to the military. The events that would unfold over the next five years still cause me to look back at them with amazement.

In my very first week back in the Air Force things got strange. I was assigned to Luke AFB in Arizona. I called in to report for duty stating that this is Sergeant DeLong reporting for duty. There is a hesitation on the phone at the other end. This was followed by a question. "Is this the Sergeant DeLong from Mountain Home"? I said, "Yes it is. Then I said, "Who is this?" He answered, "This is Joe." I said "Joe?" He declared, "Yes, Joe Shelton from Mountain Home." Joe Shelton was my supervisor when I was stationed at Mountain Home and was instrumental in training me to be his Ace Troubleshooter. I couldn't believe my luck, Here I am falling right back under his command. After coming out of the initial shock, I felt comforted knowing that I was returning to the military under someone who knows me and I know them.

In my first week, Sergeant Shelton started to assign individuals to me which is a normal thing to do because I am a

Noncommissioned Officer (NCO) and meant that I would be supervising part of the individuals in the shop. At the beginning of the second week, he called me into the shop and shocked me again by saying that I would now disregard my supervisory position in the shop and that he had a job for me working for the commander.

I'm thinking are you crazy? I've been back in the Air Force one week and you are already sending me up to work for the commander! He said, "Yes, he has a couple of situations up there that he needs help with and I believe you can take care of those situations."

Well, here we go with that label, if you will, again being put in a position of leadership. Of course, Sergeant Shelton has had some experience with me and knows my capabilities. So, I trust in that and accept the position.

I reported to the commander, and he explained that he had a situation with Training and Mobility. He showed me to my desk, and I responded, "Okay let me take a look and see what we've got."

I opened the desk drawer and pulled out two sets of inspection reports. As I went through each section, I discovered in the training and mobility area, the Squadron had never obtained more than an Unsatisfactory Rating. Wowser! My first thoughts are that I have never done training and I have no experience in mobility so what am I doing here? Well, in good military fashion, I replied, "Mine is not to ask why mine is to do or die." So I began to dig in to find out what the underlying challenges were with training. I also started to look into our Mobility commitment and why we had failed in both areas.

What I began to undercover was training requirements weren't too hard, they simply had a very large backlog of training that needed to be accomplished and had no system for making individuals aware of their training. I began to organize a "Tickler File" where I could put the individual's training. It included projected training for a particular month and day. Then all I had to do was look at that particular day and notify those individuals of their training. The result; no one missed the required training, and I didn't have to do any rescheduling. Mission accomplished.

Mobility requirements were a totally different story Their Mission as a training base was a bit different than most bases. However, the mission wasn't the problem. The problem was getting our equipment secured on pallets and loaded on an airplane to deploy wherever the Air Force needed to deploy. This was a challenge simply because I would train a pallet crew but every time we would have an exercise, Command would send me a different set of individuals. This means all of my prior crew training was in vain, and I had to start at ground zero to bring the newbies up to snuff. Therefore, Mobility could never get a pallet to pass inspection.

One day after an inspection, I am out on the flight line tearing apart our pallet. Up walks the I.G. (Inspector General), and he asks me "what are you doing here?" I am standing in the middle of this palette filled with equipment, and he doesn't understand what I am doing. I relayed to him that for some reason we can't get a pallet to pass inspection, therefore I am trying to figure out a way to do that. He exclaimed, "Ok Carry On." Somehow I knew and would find out later that there was more to this than just a chance meeting.

My solution to this problem ended up being this… I had one of those old Polaroid cameras. The ones where you would take a picture and the picture would come out the front of the camera. You would waive the picture around in the air a little bit, and the picture would instantly develop. Remember I am dyslexic and dyslexics think in pictures. I took the palette and equipment and as I put the equipment on one piece at a time, I would take a picture of the position and how the other equipment intermingled and fit in with the other pieces of equipment. I took the pictures that I developed and sequentially pasted them on a page, step by step from the beginning to the end. Then I made black and white photocopies of these pages penciling in the name of the pieces of equipment. Now I have a picture storybook of how to exactly put together the palette. I can hand this book to any crew chief and know the palette will be put together in a consistently prescribed way that will pass inspection.

Eureka! Mobility now went from an Unsatisfactory Rating to an Outstanding Rating which is the top of the ratings. The organization stayed there the rest of the time that I was there.

Remember the I.G. I talked about? He came down to the Squadron one day and asked what I had done to make such a significant difference. I pulled out three copies of my picture book and showed them to him. I showed him how I had made copies of the assembly of these pallets. I explained to him the reason for three copies was to give one copy to the palette crew and send one copy with the plane to the destination. I would keep the third copy as a master that way the equipment would be put together here wherever the mission took us, then returned in the same fashion. He asked if I could make a copy and send it to him. I said, "Sure why not." So I did. I guess Sergeant Shelton was right. I didn't know that I had what it took to solve or fix the situation, but I made it happen. I had taken the Squadron from an Unsatisfactory Rating to an Outstanding Rating, in both areas. I was proud of my accomplishment, and it taught me a lot about myself.

CHAPTER 10

Busted Tapping the Zone. An Attribute of Dyslexia

This was an Awakening for me. I had always known since I was a very young child I could see things in my head and be able to visualize them in great detail. Pursuing them, staying with them, and staying with the big picture, I was able to make things happen and make things come together. In an attempt to make this Mobility situation turn around, I was sitting in my office one day, I was leaning back in my chair, I had my hands in my lap and my eyes were closed. Now as most people know getting caught sleeping in the military is a big No-No. The way my office sat the Commander's office was down the hall to my left and the Chief's office was down the hall to my right. This is one of those old-time wooden barracks-type Office Buildings so when someone walks from point A to point B the floors are very noisy. One day I am trying to come up with a solution for this Mobility situation. I hear the Chief come out of the Commander's office and head towards his office. I am in one of these deep visualization states and I am feeling the answer to my situation is coming. It is about to emerge so I don't want to break the trance I'm in. As the chief walks by me I don't want to open my eyes but I don't want the chief to think that I'm sleeping. When the chief walks by I raise one finger just to show him I'm not sleeping. His reply was "Yeah right." In this state, the answer to my picture books did come to me. I immediately ran over to the chief's office and told him, "Hey chief I wasn't sleeping but I was on the verge of a breakthrough with this Mobility thing and I didn't want to break the trance." His reply was "yeah right if it works do it." From that point on every time the chief would walk by my desk, I would raise one finger and he would reply "yeah   right."

CHAPTER 11

It's off to Spain
I Go.

I have now received orders to Zaragoza, Spain. I am very excited about this assignment because, in my first four years, I spent a little time at this Air Force Base. I loved the country, the way of life, and the terrain. My mission now is to get my family ready to go overseas. If you don't understand what a task like this can be, well, you're not moving across town you are moving to another country. This can be very taxing on a family leaving friends, leaving school.

I arrive in Spain and have reported to my Squadron Duty Center and we are headed to our first Commander's Call. I am told by my Chief to wear my Blues. I am wondering, why my Blues. I asked the Chief what's up with the Blues. He said, "When we have new troops come in we like to have them wear their Blues so the individuals that have already been at the base for a while can welcome them." I thought okay that sounds good

When I get to the Commander's call I am sitting in a theater with the rest of the squadron, the commander walks in and calls the meeting to order. He says "I need these individuals to report to the stage." He gives out the names and I'm one of them. Now I'm wondering what's going on. We all line up on stage in the order he called us up and the commander States the first order of business is Recognition and Medals. Well, now I am shocked. I just got here! As he walks down the line, reads and presents the medal to each individual, he gets to me, he talks about my accomplishments at my previous base with training and Mobility. Now, something very unusual happens at this point. He pins the medal on my chest which is normal, we salute each other, he then leans over and says "by the way you now work for me." Wow, here we go again. From that day forward, I worked for the commander in a variety of positions.

While I was in Zaragoza Spain I discovered a talent that I had. It emerged from a hobby I was doing in Arizona. When I was in Arizona I would take a 12" by 12" piece of wood and route the insignias of the various squadrons in our wing. I then stained the various colors of the insignia in the wood to make it come to life. I made a set of these plaques for the wall in my office area. One day the commander is walking by and he stops. He is looking at these plaques… I'm thinking, uh-oh, I'm probably not supposed to have this kind of thing hanging on the wall. He looks at me in that, you're in trouble kind of look and says, "Will you make a set of these for our conference room?" Shweuuu! "Sure," I said.

About three weeks later here stands the commander again. "The Wing Commander wants to see you," he says, with the same look as before. Gulp! I report to the Wing Commander and he asks, "If I could make a set of these plaques for his office he would be happy to pay me for my time." "But of course," says I. Well, it didn't stop there… next was the base commander and finally the commander of the 8th Air Force. A Brigadier General.

After the completion of my time at Zaragoza, I discovered an exciting new talent. I had started a side business while I was stationed in Spain and it was going very well. I was very interested in taking this to a new level once back in the U.S.

Within a few months after my return to the U.S., my father became terminally ill. I would spend my days focusing on the days we had left. In November 1987 my father passed.

CHAPTER 12

This Would Become a Time of Extreme Internal Awareness.

If you are Dyslexic, people kind of stand back at a distance and say things like, "he really thinks differently, I think he might be a little crazy, you probably shouldn't do that." To some degree, this might be true to a left-brainer. Left-brainers think past and present, stay in the box, and everything must be in order (1,2,3) or it won't work. This equates to 80% of the human race. For the other 20% of us right-brainers that think present and future, out of the box (what are the possibilities), it doesn't matter what order as long as we accomplish the big picture (which we can see in great detail) this can be a little unsettling for most others.

In 1987, shortly after my father's death, I decided to test my wings and start a retail business based on my experience from my military hobbies. I started in the basement of my home in an unused room we had. My nitch... the military. Within a one-hour drive, there were six military bases and I very much understood the military language.

As my business started to grow I would have very strong dreams about my future storefront. I call them strong dreams because they were very intense and much more detailed than normal. As time would go I would change this term to visions.

One day my son and I were in a Service Merchandise getting some fishing tackle for the next day. As we exited the store I looked over to my right, particularly at one store in a strip mall and the words just popped out of my mouth "there's my store!" My son looked at me as though I was crazy. I repeated, "that's my store, I've seen it a thousand times!" I told my son to go look in the window and you will see a counter here and a window there and a machine here, drawing a little map on my hand. He goes over and looks, turns around, and looks at me with the look of astonishment and says, you're right how did you know? I said I've seen it a thousand times in my dreams. Now he's looking at me like I've had too much to drink or something.

I walked away from that experience a little shook. How could this be my store if someone else already owned it? Because we were both in the same business, different markets, I decided to go see him. My approach was because we were in different markets and he had 10 times the capabilities I had, maybe he would do some wholesale work for me.

This is where I got the shock of my life... after talking and agreeing to some wholesale work he said I have a better idea. Why don't you buy the business? After I picked my jaw off the floor, I had a bunch of questions.

Me: How long have you been here?

Al: One month.

Me: One month, why do you want to sell?

Al: I found out I have a heart condition, I need a triple bypass and I don't think I will be able to keep the store open.

Me: What are your conditions for sale?

Al: I want $50,000. I want $10,000 up front and I will carry the loan.

Me: Wowser! Seriously! Wait a minute are sure that's it?

Al: Yes, you are in the same business and I know you can make it work.

Me: Boy, I'm going to have to think about this.

Needless to say, I walked out of the store that day a little weak at the knees.

At this stage of the game, a big wrench got thrown into the mix. My mother became terminally ill with congestive heart failure. So I went to Al to tell him I probably couldn't buy the business. My mother was terminally ill and I couldn't think about much else at the time. If he could find another buyer he should go ahead and sell. He said he completely understood and to just keep him posted.

Within three months my mother had passed. Now we have to deal with an estate. So, I went back to Al and told him that my mother had passed and now we had to liquidate the estate and that was going to take some time. His response was simply ok, just keep me posted.

About a month after my mother had passed I got a call from my older sister. She said that our mother had not left her life insurance to who we had thought. At this point, all kinds of things start running through my head. My older sister, because she is physically challenged, my younger brother, because he is mentally challenged and they always say watch out for the friends a person has just before they pass. So I told my sister, "ok I'm sitting down, who was it?" She said, "You." At this point, I think my sister is messing with me. Seriously I said. She said, "Seriously you." So how much is it? $10,000.

Within the next month, that storefront in the strip mall became mine.

In the end, the store was mine. The visions were correct, I just didn't know **how** it was going to be mine.

I would spend the next 20 years there and grow from my basement to three storefronts.

What I learned from this is that **"déjà vu"** is real. This has happened so many times I've lost count.

Hint: Dyslexics/Right-Brainers **DRBs** are many times intuitive and visionary. Destined for entrepreneurship

CHAPTER 13

Severed at the Neck - PTSD

Severed at the neck is probably the best description I have heard of explaining what I am about to tell you. This was the description used by Eric Clapton when he lost his daughter. On September 13th, 2007 my life would change dramatically and forever. My daughter called to tell me that my son had died. What happened next I didn't know or could have imagined could happen to a human being. Most would call it the State of Shock but for the most part, my brain went numb. I couldn't feel anything. To give you an idea of what this might feel like in a situation you may have experienced I will describe it this way. You go to bed at night and of course, all of your arms and legs are there. You wake up the next morning and naturally take inventory. You discover that one of your arms is gone or at least you can't feel it. You know it's there but you can't move it, you can't feel it, so you roll over on your back grab what feels like a cold piece of meat pull it up over on your chest and wait. Now the feeling slowly starts to come back and many times there's a tingling feeling that goes with it. But it can take so long that many times you wonder if you may have lost your arm.

For me, my brain was numb. I could not construct or hold a thought. It's a good thing going to the bathroom is automatic because if I would have had to think about it, I would have been in big trouble. This went on for months... it was very difficult to function. And then the fear sets in, am I going to get my brain function back or is this it for the rest of my life.

CHAPTER 14

Education is the Path to Recovery

In an effort to put Humpty Dumpty back together again, I dove into researching many of the perplexing questions I'd come across in the conversations with my son and I was scared to death I'd lost that creative productive person I was.

My father having 12 heart attacks and my son passing from cardiomyopathy just about makes me a cardiologist. My father got pretty good at determining when he was going to have a heart attack. So he was able to alert us to get him to the hospital before they killed him. My son's situation with cardiomyopathy was a little different in that he had an enlarged heart. I like to say he had a big heart because he did. There weren't a lot of options available for my son and some of the options seemed a bit paradoxal. Something my son said that kind of set me back was "dad I don't think I can live with someone else's heart in me." I wasn't sure exactly what he knew about the heart and its functions other than a pump. The other problem with a heart transplant is the prognosis for cardiomyopathy is 18 to 24 months and the heart transplant list has a three-year wait

Let me explain some of the Mysteries connected with the Heart. If you do any kind of research on the heart you will find some amazing things like the heart has memory. There are thousands of documented cases where the recipient of a heart transplant took on many of the characteristics of the donor. The heart has its own little brain. The electromagnetic (EM) wave of the heart-brain can be measured across a room. More information is sent from the heart to the brain through the Vagus Nerve, than the other way around. The heart starts beating on its own some two weeks before our brain starts to develop.

This brings me to another discovery when it comes to our brains. With current science, if we break it down it appears we have 5 brains. A left-brain (LB), a right-brain (RB), a primitive brain, an evolutionary brain, and a heart-brain (HB). Certain characteristics fall into each brain. The most important is that of the heart-brain. It can be measured and emits an EM Wave 5000 times stronger than the cranial brain. It can override the brain in our head. You know those gut feelings you get? Vagus Nerve!

So that you might have a better understanding of what is where, here is a breakdown of LB, RB, and HB.

CHAPTER 15

Heart-Brain Characteristics

Heart-Brain characteristics are seated in Emotions and Compassion. There are lists as high as **"121 emotions"**, however, the **Six Basic Emotions are:**

Love - Joy - Surprise - Anger - Sadness – Fear

Emotions are more powerful than thoughts and Emotions can override thought.

Left-Brain – Right-Brain
LEFT BRAIN people tend to:

Use logic
Detail oriented

Facts rule
Words and language
Present and Past
Math and science
Can comprehend
Knowing
Acknowledges
Order/pattern perception
Knows object name
Reality-Based
Forms strategies
Practical
Safe
In-the-box thinker
Analytical
Sequential
Rational

Left Brainers show greater ability in:
Language skills,
Skilled movement,
Analytical time sequence processing.

**Left Brainers seem more suited to
Careers in:**

- Law,
- Accounting,
- Science.

RIGHT BRAIN people tend to:

Uses feeling

"Big picture" oriented

Imagination rules

Symbols and images (Pictorial)

Present and future

Philosophy & Religion

Can "get it" (i.e. meaning)

Believes

Appreciates

Spatial perception

Knows object function

Fantasy based

Presents possibilities

Impetuous

Risk-taking

Out-of-the-box thinker

Interpersonal

Random

Intuitive

Right Brainers show greater ability in:

Copying of designs,
Discrimination of shapes e.g. picking out a
camouflaged object,
Understanding geometric properties,
Reading faces,
Music,
Global holistic processing,
Understanding of metaphors,
Expressing emotions,
Reading emotions

**Right Brainers seem more suited to
Careers in:**

- Entrepreneurship,
- Athletics,
- Sales,
- Art,
- Music,
- Crafts,
- Dancing.

CHAPTER 16

Is Dyslexia a Gift or a Detriment?

"Left Hander's think in their Right Mind.

&

Right Hander's think in what's Left,"
~ Mike DeLong

Do you have a Black Sheep in your family? Is your child not doing well in English, Spelling, or Math? Do you feel your child has an overactive imagination, and daydreams a lot? Does your child show signs of dyslexia? OR… ARE YOU THAT PERSON? Do you feel as though the world sees you as less intelligent, yet you find yourself saying "I told you so?"

Any friction between you and your boss or vice-versa? Feel like you are standing at opposite ends of the building saying "they just don't get it?" How about your marriage?

Imagine going through life and every day you do 500 reps with a 10 lb. dumbbell, but you only do those reps with your right arm. To say the least, you are going to look a little odd to the rest of the world, and they might be asking you how you got to look that way. That's not normal or is it?

This concept alone, or at least knowing the difference, made Howard Hughes i.e. Hughes Industries very wealthy. And all you want to do is get along with your child or your parents...

Understanding the difference is liberating! It can save you thousands of dollars in psychotherapy expenses! It can turn your working relationship or your marriage into a dream team!

IT'S NOT RIGHT OR WRONG, BETTER OR WORSE, IT'S JUST HOW WE PROCESS INFORMATION. WHICH SIDE DOES WHAT, WHICH SIDE IS YOUR DOMINATE SIDE, AND KNOWING THE DIFFERENCE!

"We have a DiFF-order or a DiFF-ability." That is, dyslexics process information **DIFFERENTLY** and they access **DIFFERENT** areas of their brains that most others would not.

CHAPTER 17

Languaging is Like Going to the Library

Why is this? Well, think of it this way, the language skills are at the library, and the library is located in our left-brain. So, when we right-brainers want to say something we must go to the library (LB) and that takes a little time (hence the pause), and as I am sure you have sometimes all experienced that the library is closed.

Here is the real difficulty.

Dyslexics have difficulty reading. Out loud is worse!!!! Whoever invented grammar and spell-checker had us dyslexics in mind.

Can you read this sentence?

.

The above illustration should read as: "The President of the United States is leaving for the White House."

However, the earlier picture example shows how the above sentence would look to a dyslexic. We think in pictures as opposed to words. Part of the hesitation in our speech is we have to create the picture first, and then we describe it. If there is a word that doesn't have a good picture attached to it then we stall.

We have difficulties with tests. Dyslexics are experiential learners. That means this, we take the test first then we go back and figure out the answers.

Dyslexics have memory problems… we just can't remember what they are.

Sounds pretty bleak right? Well, let me add one more iron to the fire. I'm left-handed. That means my predominant side is controlled by my right brain. This can add an extra level of difficulty for the DRB to contend with.

If you are a left-handed dyslexic, which many are, this complicates things.

Is there such a thing as a left-handed pencil?

Grab a pencil with your favorite brand on it. Put the pencil in your right hand and sign your name.

Now put the pencil in your left hand and sign your name.

A little or a lot uncomfortable isn't it?

One more time I ask you, do you think there is such a thing as a Left handed pencil?

Make sure the pencil is in your left hand... like you were about to write with it...

Now Read the label.

What's wrong with that picture?

Yes, there is such a thing as a left-handed pencil!

If you have ever heard left-handers are more intelligent, well consider this... left-handers have to do everything twice, right-handed by design, and then translate that to left-handed. What this means is left-handers have to use more of both sides of their brains to accomplish a mission. Dyslexics are very much the same way.

CHAPTER 18

How can Dyslexia Possibly be a Gift?

Well, let me offer some of the positive characteristics of dyslexia or being a right-brainer:

- Left-handers think in their right minds and right-handers think in what's left.

- Dyslexics are highly intuitive - known to have "street smarts." They are often "dead on" in judging the personalities of others.

- Many can sense emotions and the energy of others.

- They at times appear to zone out… that is because we know where the zone is.

- They have vivid imaginations (we are very creative)

- They see the big picture.

I have to **stop right here** and explain something about me. At some point in time, you may ask me a question and I will respond "**I don't care**".

Now, this goes way back to a **fishing strategy** of mine. I would go fishing with my friends and they would ask me, almost in anger, how do you catch so many fish? After some pondering, I came to this. **I don't care!**

When I'm fishing, I couldn't care less if I am catching fish. There is a bigger picture here; the sound of the river, the cool mountain air, and most of all God's Tapestry surrounding me.

I think the fish just bite on my line to distract me.

So when I say I don't care, **it is not that I am not heartfelt.** It is that there is a bigger picture here.

Dyslexics think outside the box... as in *what are the possibilities here*?

They can handle random. Non-dyslexics might call this multitasking; however, a human cannot multitask.

Humans can only hold one thought at a time. However, dyslexics can switch at lightning speed. Dyslexics just don't care what order thoughts come in.

Dyslexics display an extreme work ethic. 'Highly successful/overachiever'; Wow, I've never been accused of that before. Ha Ha!

CHAPTER 19

8 Common Characteristics of Dyslexia

1. Can utilize the brain's ability to alter and create perceptions (the primary ability).
2. Are highly aware of the environment.
3. Are more curious than average.
4. Can think mainly in pictures instead of words.
5. Are highly intuitive and insightful.
6. Can think and perceive multi-dimensionally (using all the senses).
7. Can experience thought as reality.
8. Have vivid imaginations.

CHAPTER 20

A statement from the International Dyslexia Association

"Although dyslexics may struggle with reading, writing, spelling and even math, many dyslexics excel in their outside the box thinking, vision, leadership, oral skills and ability to lead and inspire. Wow!

They thrive in careers where visual-spatial and or kinesthetic talents can be realized: For example - Entrepreneurs, Engineers, Trades like (carpentry, plumbing, electrical), Artisans, Interior Decorators, Actors, Musicians, Police/Investigators, Athletes, and Business Executives (CEOs) usually with staff or assistants i.e. a room full of left-brainers."

So, I once pondered, who else the world might know, has excelled or not, with an altered brain function similar to mine?

This got a little scary because what if a serial killer's name popped up?

Neural Signature for Dyslexia:
Disruption of Posterior Reading Systems

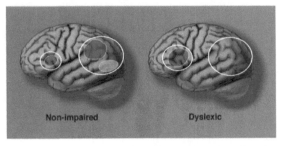

© Sally Shaywitz, *Overcoming Dyslexia*, 2003

I'm in good company.

Here are a few of the dyslexic people that you might know. Thomas Edison, Henry Ford, Alexander Graham Bell, F.W. Woolworth, Walt Disney, Nelson Rockefeller, Richard Branson, William Hewlett (HP), Steve Jobs, Bill Gates, Charles Schwab, Steven Spielberg, Tommy Hilfiger, Ted Turner, and Cisco CEO John Chambers.

To me, dyslexia has been a blessing even if I do think 'Bass Ackwards.'

I have friends that are real Fart Smellers.

We shouldn't be ridiculed because we are Teople Poo.

Here is an extended list of famous Dyslexics.

Hans Christian Andersen

Harry Belafonte

Alexander Graham Bell

George Hums

Stephen J. Cannell

Cher

Winston Churchill

Leonardo da Vinci

Wall Disney

Albert Einstein

Henry Ford

Danny Glover

Steve Jobs

F.W. Woolworth

Richard Branson

Steven Spielberg

Ted Turner

Sir Isaac Newton

Brian Tracy

Sir Anthony Hopkins

Whoopi Goldberg

Bruce Jenner

William Lear

Jay Leno

Greg Louganis

General George Patton

Nelson Rockefeller

Charles Schwab

Jackie Stewart

Quentin Tarantino

Woodrow Wilson

W. H. Yeats

Thomas Edison

William Hewlett

Bill Gates

Tommy Hilfiger

Cisco CEO John Chambers

Paul Orfalea (Kinko's)

Keanu Reeves

These individuals succeeded, not in spite of dyslexia, but because of it!

CHAPTER 21

What is the Paradox?

Dyslexia is a deficiency in the brain according to standards set by the majority. Shown in this image, you can see how a part of the dyslexic brain is missing, dysfunctional, or disconnected. This condition occurs in approximately 20% of the population.

The nature of the brain is to find an answer anywhere it can. What happens in this situation is it does just that by accessing both sides of the brain, left and right. Anything that can help retrieve words.

On the right side, we have pictures. Dyslexics rely heavily on pictures. As we saw in the previous example of a sentence if there is not a picture of a word such as "the", "is", or "if", then, we are in trouble. Languaging stalls us out when reading, especially reading out loud. This causes the stress to go way up because everybody is listening and watching. At this point, the brain can start to shut down. Imagine a day at school like this (I experienced this many times in my early years).

However, accessing the right side of the brain opens up many other highly useful areas. Intuition, imagination, creativity, out-of-the-box thinking.

Handling emotions is another interesting response for dyslexics. These are first processed by the heart brain then experienced by the right brain. Then the mental games begin.

CHAPTER 22

How Can Your Dyslexic Child Be Gifted?

"How can your child be gifted if they can't read and get poor grades?" ~ *Statement from a Grade School Principal* – Ouch!

And this reaction by teachers and administrators which I know too well; "He's a smart kid, he's just too lazy."

When parents hear the above statements, they have to wonder how in the world can a Dyslexic Child be Gifted.

As a child, for me, going to school felt more like a prison sentence than an education. School academics were painful, confining, restricting... "HELL," to say the least. I did understand that at some level I

needed some kind of education to function
in   the   world.

CHAPTER 23

A word to parents.

"Parents are the ultimate role models for children. Every word, movement, and action has an effect. No other person or outside force has a greater influence on a child than the parent." ~ Bob Keeshan

Don't Freak Out! There are thousands upon thousands of stories of Dyslexics coming into their own after their schooling. I am one of them.

Dyslexia is a strange thing to understand for a non-dyslexic. As we start our journey through life we are given four brains to work with. The Heart-Brain, which is an actual brain attached to our hearts, a Primal-Brain, responsible for keeping us alive (fight or flight), a Left-Brain and a Right-Brain.

The Left-Brain and Right-Brain are responsible for certain areas of thinking well illustrated below:

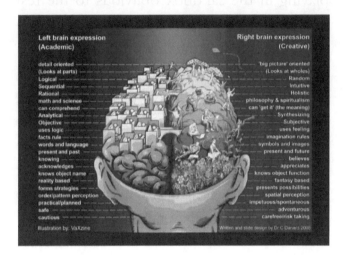

Looking at this illustration you can see where certain areas handle various types of information.

Notice on the left side you will see an area called "Words and Language." on the right side, you will see an area called "Imagination Rules and Symbols and Images."

As a newborn child, we don't have a lot of inventory in our "words and language" area. However, the "imagination" side is ready to roll. It has no boundaries and it has no rules. I'm sure you've seen the little child playing in the sandbox oblivious to the rest of the world. I have never seen one sitting in a sandbox reading the dictionary.

For about the first five years of our lives, this is when we draw from the creative side to create our daily lives. If it feels good, we do it. All the while we are developing our AUDIO language skills. Why it is easier to learn how to walk than talk.

THEN it happens early in our education… someone draws a line in the sand and says, "We will teach your children how to read and write. This is our standard"; then more lines are drawn in the sand. "Those of you who get it in our predetermined time stand here on the left and those of you that don't get it in our predetermined time, stand here on the right."

Measuring sticks, we can't live and evolve as a species without them. We measure everything and then we begin to divide based on what we measured. Where I feel we fail ourselves, particularly in the area of Dyslexia is we take nearly 20% of our population and call them defective, disabled, diseased, or worse.

I find it fascinating that in those 20%, there are individuals like,

Hans Christian Anderson	*Whoopi Goldberg*
Harry Belafonte	*Bruce Jenner*
Alexander Graham Bell	*William Lear*
George Hums	*Jay Leno*
Stephen J. Cannell	*Greg Louganis*
Cher	*General George Patton*
Winston Churchill	*Nelson Rockefeller*
Leonardo de Vinci	*Charles Schwab*
Walt Disney	*Jackie Stewart*
Albert Einstein	*Quentin Tarantino*
Henry Ford	*Woodrow Wilson*
Danny Glover	*W. H. Yeats*
Steve Jobs	*Thomas Edison*
F. W. Woolworth	*William Hewlett*
Richard Branson	*Bill Gates*
Steven Spielberg	*Tommy Hilfiger*
Ted Turner	*Cisco CEO JohnChambers*
Sir Isaac Newton	*Paul Orfalea (Kinko's)*
Brian Tracy	*Keanu Reeves*
Sir Anthony Hopkins	

Imagine what our world might look like if these individuals had allowed themselves to be confined by lines in the sand. We might not have lightbulbs, automobiles, phones or cell phones, computers, or a language to operate them, just to name a few.

As we begin our schooling around four or five years of age, we have entered the land of measuring sticks whether it's academics, athletics, or the arts; there is a measuring stick. As children, we know nothing of the measuring sticks. We, in heart, are there to be recognized for our efforts and very willing to earn them.

You might see early signs in your child, like,

- Often mispronounces words, like saying "beddy tear" instead of "teddy bear."

- Was considered by his doctor to be a "late talker"

- Often has trouble naming familiar objects, saying general words like *thing* and *stuff* instead of the names of objects.

- Has trouble learning a new word, even after you've tried to teach it to him many times.

- Has trouble learning nursery rhymes or song lyrics that rhyme, and has difficulty recognizing and producing rhymes.

- Has trouble remembering sequences, such as singing the letters of the alphabet or saying the days of the week in the right order.

- Has difficulty learning letter names and remembering the sounds they make.

- Confuses letters that look similar (B, D, P, Q),

- Struggles to read familiar words (like CAT or THE) especially when there are no pictures or other context clues; often skips over or

confuses small words
like "TO" and "AS" when reading
aloud.

- Often tells stories that are hard to follow; has trouble talking about an event in a logical order.

- Can't point out his own name and has trouble writing it.

This is a short list and any of them by themselves is not cause for concern. However, if you see many of these together, it is time to pay more attention. Make teachers aware of your observations. Start documenting your findings, conversations, and meetings. Save homework and other documents that support your concerns. Start an IEP (Individual Education Program) notebook. You can get one at www.mikedelonginternational.com

CHAPTER 24

Where are the Gifts?

To help understand the gifts of Dyslexia think of it this way… you have a left hand and you have a right hand, a left leg and a right leg, a left eye and a right eye and so on… in all of these lefts and rights, we have a predominant side. We are left-handed or right-handed. This doesn't mean we only use one hand. We use both hands. However, one side functions a little better than the other. This is our predominate side. If you were injured, say your right hand, you would use your left hand more to accomplish what you needed to do. The same goes for our left and right brains.

Dyslexics have a deficiency on the left side of their brain, a weak spot if you will. This might be like being born missing two fingers on one hand. You can still use that hand, it just has a little different capability than the majority of the people in the world that have all their fingers. This forces them to use the other side or areas of their brain to solve the task at hand. No Pun Intended.

Referring back to the illustration of the left and right brain, you will see on the right side where many of these gifts reside.

This is not to say this is the only side we use anymore or less than a left-brainer. However, because of the characteristics of dyslexia, we are forced to go to the right-brain to find solutions while the left-brain world keeps us very busy on the left.

Here are some of the gifts explained.

CHAPTER 25

Big Picture Thinkers vs Detailed Thinkers

The best way I can explain this is to visualize a jigsaw puzzle. When you look at the box top you see the puzzle in its completed form or the big picture. However, to complete the big picture there are a lot of detailed pieces that have to be put in place. Dyslexics and Right-brainers are better at holding the big picture in their heads and not getting lost in the details. In my section on *Busted Tapping the Zone,* this is exactly what I'm talking about. I could see what needed to happen, I just needed the right set of pieces to complete the puzzle.

Here are some of some of the things that can cause friction between a DRB Dyslexic/Right-Brainer and a Left-Brainer.

The **big picture** people tend to be creative, strategic, and visionary… they can be messy, disorganized, and forgetful. On the other hand, **detail-oriented** people are conscientious and demanding… they can lack perspective or fail to prioritize. These two types tend to complement each other and work together very well.

15 Struggles Only Big-Picture Thinkers Will Understand

By Heidi Priebe, May 15th 2015

Big-picture thinkers are creative, innovative, and highly perceptive of patterns and connections in their environment. But it's not all fun and games. Big-picture thinkers encounter a great deal of resistance in their day-to-day lives – if many of the struggles listed below apply to you, chances are you are one.

1. The devil isn't in the details – the devil *is* the details.

You don't understand why every "I" has to be dotted and every "T" has to be crossed – if the general idea is apparent, why stress over the specifics? Neurotic people are going to be the death of you.

2. The ends tend to justify the means for you – which others don't always understand.

You have to break a few eggs to make an omelet, okay. No matter how many people question what you're doing, it's always part of a bigger plan. Just wait and see…

3. You are constantly being told to "Be realistic."

That is just about the worst advice you could possibly think of. Were the Wright brothers being realistic? No. And that's why we now have airplanes.

4. Your eyes are often bigger than your stomach.

From time to time your ambitions get away from you, and you have trouble reeling them back in. How did you end up working

70 hours a week? There was a project proposal four months ago; you remember that much…

5. You end up doing many things alone.

"Wow that sounds like a cool plan!" This is something that you hear a lot.

"Wow, I'll go with your plan!" Is something that you almost never hear. Other people are entertained by your schemes but not necessarily on board for them. Good thing you're comfortable trying new things alone…

6. Studying a highly concentrated topic makes you want to cry.

You get the general idea – so why must you learn every excruciating detail about where and when the project took place? That doesn't matter. You are more interested in whether you learn something that matters now?

7. When detail-oriented people want nothing more than to shoot holes in your exciting new idea.

You want to plaster a huge sign to your forehead that says "THE DETAILS WILL WORK THEMSELVES OUT." Because they will if you're smart about getting around them. And you are. People who see details first, ideas second, drive you insane.

8. You get tired of following through on plans.

The grunt work involved in actually following up on a plan is torturous to you. Your dream job is one where you have underlings to do such work. And you're just the idea generator.

9. Conversely, people are surprised when you do follow through on a grandiose plan.

You told them you were going to do this five hundred times. Why were they surprised when you actually did it?

10. You find menial jobs surprisingly difficult, but high-pressure jobs surprisingly easy.

Administrative tasks have never been your strong suit. But put you in a fast-paced environment where tough decisions have to be made on the fly and you're thriving.

11. You tend to be a bit argumentative – but it's not out of spite.

You're quick to analyze the overall principle of what someone's saying and notice holes in their reasoning – and it only makes sense to point them out. Why continue to have a conversation if the basis of discussion is invalid? Unfortunately, the person you're talking to doesn't always see it that way.

12. You often fail to notice things that are right in front of you.

Big-picture thinkers are the masters of losing the keys they were actually holding. Or not noticing the dent on their car until it's been there for a month (and someone else points it out). So a few things don't make it onto the radar. Oh well…

13. You've been accused of lacking common sense.

And that doesn't really offend you. Common sense is for commoners.

14. You see everything as it could be rather than as it is.

You have a tendency to stick with projects, ideas, even relationships, long after they've gone under because you see their potential first and their reality second.

15. Your optimism occasionally exceeds your abilities – but you wouldn't have it any other way.

Some of your ideas are a little too out there to work, but that's okay. In the end, you value the ideas themselves over their practical application. Speculation is your sport – and you can't win every game you play.

CHAPTER 26

Advantages of Big Picture Thinking

There are many advantages to being a big-picture thinker:

1. You are motivated. You see the opportunity, and you are willing to get the support you need to make your dream a reality.
2. You have lots of ideas. You continuously have new ideas in your mind. In fact, it can be challenging to stay focused on one because there are so many!
3. You don't see problems. You can quickly come up with solutions to potential obstacles and are fast at solving problems.
4. You see big possibilities. Big-picture thinkers think *big*. You can see the big picture - potentially, financially or otherwise - of the plans and get very

excited about how an idea could play out.

Detail-oriented thinking is a more precise way of planning, organizing, and managing activities with specific details. Detail-oriented people are not visionaries but are very good at executing the details of a plan. They likely overthink things in the process of organizing the plans. Detail-oriented people often are considered lacking in common sense because they may not fully comprehend how all of the various pieces of a project. They are focused on the narrow area they are working on. "Analysis Paralysis" – so caught up in the details that you lose sight of the big picture.

CHAPTER 27

Intuitive vs Analytical Thinking

Because DRB's Dyslexics/Right-Brainers are inclined to be more intuitive they seem like they are dreamers, like they are out of touch with reality. However, they can visualize in a 3D or holographic way, based on their intuition, how many different components will come together to make the Big Picture work. If one is an analytical type who is inclined to deal with facts only, then DRBs can seem like they are just crazy.

In the section on *A Time of Extreme Internal Awareness,* I found intuition right in front of my face. We describe this in many ways; I had a dream about this, I had a gut feeling this was going to happen, I just knew it. Where DRBs seem like they are a little crazy to others is when they learn to trust these impressions. If the situation isn't totally clear in the beginning, we know we will get more pieces in the future that will put the whole picture in order.

According to Canadian psychologist Gordon Pennycook and his colleagues, all of us are intuitive thinkers. As we solve problems and make decisions in our daily lives, we let our emotions guide us. And that's a good thing because our "gut feelings" have been honed over evolutionary history to help us quickly and effortlessly achieve good enough outcomes.

Take ordering a meal at a restaurant as an example. You look over the menu, find something appealing, and order it. If you attempted a rational decision-making process, in this case, you'd get stuck in "paralysis by analysis"—unable to make a choice.

Yet, there are cases where intuitions will lead us astray. Because intuitive thinking is the default mode for humans, most people respond with a "quick and dirty" response that gets the answer wrong. However, as Pennycook and his colleagues point out, some of us are willing to expend the effort to think analytically.

It's important not to think of intuitive and analytical thinkers as two different types of people since all of us are capable of both modes of reasoning. Some people are more in the habit of thinking analytically. People in the STEM (science, technology, engineering, and math) fields have years of training in analytical thinking. But even these people can be led astray by their intuitions, especially when working on problems outside their area of expertise. Likewise, even highly intuitive people can be coaxed into thinking analytically under the right circumstances.

There are significant life consequences for people who are willing to engage in analytical thought processes. Religion is a good example. All religious faiths are based on intuitions. We're indoctrinated with the beliefs and practices of our particular religion early in childhood, accepting these teachings as obvious truths. Yet those who are willing to think analytically quickly spot the logical inconsistencies in religious tenets, and they question their childhood faith.

More generally, people who habitually engage in analytical thinking also tend to be more skeptical toward paranormal claims and supernatural beliefs. They're also more likely to question claims that, while not supernatural, still don't reconcile well with a logical, materialistic worldview. For example, they question conspiracy theories, which are usually more complicated than standard explanations. Likewise, they take a dubious stance toward alternative medicine.

Analytical thinking also affects people's moral attitudes. All of us have an innate moral sense that we share with our primate cousins and perhaps other mammals as well. When we put these rules of behavior into words, they're usually phrased as "shoulds" and "shouldn'ts."

As far as an innate moral sense is concerned, "shoulds" typically invoke emotions that compel us to cooperate with family and friends. Psychologists refer to this urge-to-help intuition as "pro-sociality" because it's the backbone of primate— including human—social behavior.

Pennycook and his colleagues found that people who mainly engage in intuitive thinking are more likely to help out, even at a considerable cost to themselves. People who think analytically aren't necessarily selfish or greedy. However, in social exchanges, they tend to evaluate the potential payoffs to themselves and others, and they gladly help when it benefits others more than it costs them.

The "shouldn'ts" of our innate moral sense are mainly derived from the more evolutionarily ancient emotion of disgust. We experience disgust in the presence of things like feces, vomit, blood, and other bodily fluids because these are all substances that carry disease. Thus, disgust is an automatic response to things that can cause sickness.

While some things are universally disgusting, we can also learn to feel disgust for items that have made us ill in the past. For me, it's peanut butter. Even the smell makes me retch.

People who are guided by their intuitive morality tend to deem behaviors that they find disgusting to be immoral for everyone. For example, a heterosexual male may deem homosexuality immoral because he finds the thought of himself engaging in such an act disgusting.

People in the habit of thinking analytically, however, tend to make moral judgments in terms of the question: "What's the harm?" If the behavior hurts no one, then it is moral. Thus, analytical thinkers will see nothing immoral about homosexual acts by consenting adults. By the same token, discrimination against same-sex marriage is seen as harmful, since it deprives these couples of legal and economic rights that are granted to heterosexual unions.

In just a couple of decades, American popular opinion on same-sex unions shifted from overwhelmingly negative to overwhelmingly positive. I suspect this is because many Americans were coaxed into thinking analytically about the issue and asking themselves, "What's the harm?" https://www.psychologytoday.com/blog/talking-apes/201602/are-you-intuitive-or-analytical-thinker

CHAPTER 28

Holistic vs Rational

Contrasting approaches

By and large DRBs will struggle the most in this area. DRBs are holistic by nature and can suffer in a completely rational environment. That is to say in this day and age the corporate environment is still very autocratic and very linear. To a DRB this is confining and can be very uncomfortable.

DRBs are big-picture thinkers and that goes the same for all that they do. They will quickly point out the holistic value or how something will affect something or someone in the long run. Playing the devil's advocate can be tortuous.

When complicated decisions have to be made — whether about salaries, layoffs, or growth strategy — executives often rely on their underlying values to help them sort through possible options. Profit maximization and rationality form the basis of one such set of values; many leaders follow this approach. Some, however, employ a more holistic approach. They believe that a company's strength can manifest itself in any number of ways and that firm value is derived from socially complex resources and relationships. New research from the W. P. Carey School of Business shows that "holistic" decision-making may create better long-term results for a company than the more traditional "rational" approach.

By definition, these two approaches (rational vs. holistic) to decision-making are wildly different.

"Rational" managers believe that precise ends should be sought through precise and calculated means. Supporters of the rational approach believe "the best method for attaining this desired outcome is by focusing their attention on quantifiable activities that can be observed and measured. In this way, the uncertainties associated with opportunistic behaviors and the environment can be managed." It is a logical, sensible approach — and one that many executives seem to believe in.

In his paper, "Rational Versus Holistic Values as a Basis for Leadership," Washburn and co-authors make the case that managers who are guided by financial statements alone (practitioners of the rational approach) are more likely to be viewed as "autocratic" and uninspiring by their subordinates. In contrast, leaders who take a more "holistic" approach — a style characterized by attention to multiple factors, including relationships — are seen as "visionary." It is these "holistic" managers, Washburn says, not their by-the-numbers counterparts, who are more likely to have a positive impact on their organizations by fostering a greater sense of employee optimism and improving overall firm performance. This paper is the first to show that "holistic" decision-making may create better long-term results for a company than the more traditional "rational" approach.

Given the pressures of the modern business environment, and the fact that the rational approach has been considered the standard among academics for so long, that makes sense: The rational approach is one that uses profit maximization as the guiding principle and so Wall Street, at least, surely supports it.

Holistic managers, meanwhile, are a bit more complicated. These executives look beyond the bottom line and believe a company's strength can manifest itself in any number of ways. Supporters of the holistic approach say "firm value is derived from socially complex resources and relationships." Critics, meanwhile, deride this approach as inexact and lament the fact that it provides no quantifiable means of finding the "right" decision.

But Washburn sees value in the holistic approach, which he says can allow executives to look at the big picture, rather than just the bottom line. He writes: "More than quantification and rational decision making, the role of the executive requires holistic consideration of resources and relationships. … So while improving performance may still be the goal, the implication for executive decision-making is to more generally focus on building core processes that could potentially add value to the organization in the long run."

In other words, Washburn believes even though holistic executives are not basing their decisions on the bottom line — as the rational side would prefer — the holistic approach can still be effective because of its broader positive implications.

The point, Washburn says, is that executives aren't just decision-makers. They are leaders, and being a leader involves a great deal more than simply deciding among options. It also involves inspiring confidence among staff, getting the most out of employees, and getting people to go the extra mile for the company.

"We proposed that if you're a rational decision maker, there will be negative influences, not necessarily on your decision making, but on the leadership you exhibit — and people aren't going to like you as well," Washburn says. "But if you're this more holistic person, where you take into account the different relationships you have with other employees, then you're going to come across as a much better person. It's a pretty simple idea."

- Many management strategy theorists believe in an economics-based view of management in which profit maximization is the guiding principle for decision making.

- Executives who follow this "rational" style of management believe that precise ends should be sought through precise and calculated means.

- A "holistic" approach, in contrast, takes into account any number of different factors. These managers believe firm value is derived from "socially complex resources and relationships," and they better understand the impact of their decisions on the overall culture of their company.

- Results from a new study show that holistic managers are viewed as less autocratic and more visionary than their rational counterparts. The study also showed holistic managers had a more positive effect on overall firm performance.
https://research.wpcarey.asu.edu/ration al-versus-holistic-two-very-different-approaches-to-executive-decision-making/

DRBs are prone to leadership and I hope you are starting to see why. We are visionaries and we are looking for solutions that benefit all involved. Henry Ford revolutionized the automotive industry with this concept. He created an affordable automobile through mass production and then turned the profits back into his employees. Powerful and very holistic.

CHAPTER 29

Philosophy vs Science

DRBs will be more philosophical. They will come from the perspective of what are the possibilities as opposed to what has been proven. Left-Brainers lean to the past and present whereas a Right-Brainer will lean to the present and future.

Let's go back a bit in history. Mankind believed on one side, the essence of man was controlled by the heart and on the other side, by the brain.

Fast forward to today… Now let's back up 20 years… they were right. In more ancient history somehow they knew… intuitively… the heart was the controller but they didn't have the scientific capabilities to prove it. Science now, in the last 20 years is showing this to be correct.

The first impressions we get of any thought start in the heart i.e. the Little Heart

Brain. Man's heart is not just a pump, even though a miraculous one it is, it has its own little brain. Case and point, if the brain is so essential to human functioning, why is it that in an embryo the heart develops and starts beating on its own, two weeks before the brain starts to develop?

Philosophy will encompass many areas of knowledge and reasoning whereas science will be more finite in structure.

CHAPTER 30

Synthesizing vs Analytical

Analytical thinking allows us to take apart any particular situation. Break it into smaller pieces. When we do this we tend to lose sight of the interactions between the smaller pieces. This is how we end up with analysis paralysis and many times lose sight of the big picture.

Synthetic thinking is making sense of the interactions – a cognitive tool for making sense of how things work together. That tool is synthesis – seeing how things work together. Synthesis is more than putting things back together again after you've taken them apart; It's understanding how things work together and maintaining the big-picture vision.

http://www.pathways.cu.edu.eg/sub pages/downloads/Analytical_Chapter_2. pdf

DRBs being big-picture thinkers will typically create the big picture and then back engineer it. Starting from the top down instead of the bottom up.

When starting from the bottom up it is easy to lose sight of the big picture. "So why was I doing all this?" When you start with the end in mind you are looking for the things you need to support the big picture and can see the synthesis of the smaller components.

In my section on *Back in (Very Strange)* I had all the pieces to the puzzle however, they weren't working together. I'm not talking about people not working together, but more like having a gear in a transmission that is the wrong ratio and it is inhibiting the performance of the engine. Creating the picture book was simply a gear of a different ratio that completely changed the dynamics of the situation for the better.

CHAPTER 31

Subjective vs Objective

Anything *objective* sticks to the facts, but anything *subjective* has feelings. *Objective* and *subjective* are opposites. *Objective*: It is raining. *Subjective*: I love the rain!

Objective is a busy word and that's a fact. An *objective* is a goal, but to be *objective* is to be unbiased. If you're *objective* about something, you have no personal feelings about it. In grammar land, *objective* relates to the object of a sentence. Anyway, people often try to be *objective*, but it's easier for robots.

Subjective, on the other hand, has feelings. Anything *subjective* is subject to interpretation. In grammar land, this word relates to the subject of the sentence. Usually, *subjective* means influenced by emotions or opinions. Humans are a *subjective* bunch and we like it that way!

https://www.vocabulary.com/articles /chooseyourwords/objective-subjective/

Because DRBs are holistic they will be more subjective. Instead of accepting a traditional view and removing their feelings, they will invoke their feelings. "How will this decision affect others in the future?" and can there be a compromise that suits both sides?

I came across this situation in a very unusual way. In my military career, there was a time when I was given an assignment. I was assigned several individuals and 90 pieces of equipment that had to be cleaned and inspected in 30 days.

The problem with this situation was too much equipment, not enough people, and too little time. It was doable, but it was going to be tight.

My strategy was to motivate the individuals as best I could with the resources I had available to me. In the military, the resources are very limited. You can't give someone a bonus in their paycheck or hand out free dinners. But you can give them an extra day off or a 3-day pass. Weekends are very important to a soldier.

I started by giving them a choice of three different work schedules.

1. 12-hour shifts 7 days a week until we are done.
2. 12-hour shifts 6 days a week and I would pick their day off.
3. 10-hour shifts, weekends off. I reserved the right to increase the hours in shifts and take away weekends if it didn't appear we were going to make it on time. Also, the sooner we get done I can start handing out 3-day passes and give additional days off.

This is called the magician's option, meaning, I already knew which one they were going to pick and the magic begins when they start to work. They work hard and make the best use of their time including dividing up the work into components for the highest efficiency.

General George Patton said, *"Don't tell them how to do something, tell them what needs to be done and let them amaze you with their ingenuity."*

Pretty cool huh? Well, my supervisor didn't think so. He said "Those are soldiers out there and you have to tell them what to do, not give them choices" and… this situation would be reflected in my performance report. Ok, I lost about 30 seconds of sleep over that one.

Come to find out what my supervisor didn't like was the fact that my approach got things done a couple of days early. The guys worked hard and intelligently. His way "12-hour shifts 7 days a week" the guys would make him sweat right to the last minute and then he was very stingy with his three-day passes.

The moral to my story is, if you treat people like they are stupid they become stupid people. If you treat people like they are intelligent you get intelligent people. Keeping people's feelings in mind will always work in your favor.

CHAPTER 32

Imagination vs Facts

Is it true that imagination is more important than knowledge?

Albert Einstein certainly thought so. He said: *"I'm enough of an artist to draw freely on my imagination, which I think is more important than knowledge. Knowledge is limited. Imagination encircles the world."*

Knowledge and imagination are enemies or independent strands in the web of our mental lives. The Oxford English Dictionary states that imagination involves "forming a mental concept of what is not actually present to the senses". Imagination is something more than memory, something novel: adding a movie star or picturing the guests without their clothes.

"Imagine we could put a man in a capsule and send them to the moon." There was a time in history when making a statement like this could get you locked up.

The word *Imagination* has haunted me since I was a kid. I referenced a statement in the section *"Something is Wrong with This Kid"* that directly relates to imagination. "Quit your dreaming and pay attention." Well, I thought I was. Inside your head is where imagination flows. In my head, there is an IMAX theater and I can play any movie I want to IMAGINE

When I hear the statement there is nothing that proves that to be true, it makes me cringe. It means to me that someone is very closed-minded and has no imagination.

Imagination is the door to the future and it takes a bit of courage to walk through it.

DRBs are good at this.

CHAPTER 33

Images vs Words

If a picture is worth a thousand words, why would I ever write anything?

Retailers and brands are already aware that visual content is a valuable tool and sharing it is important for their brand awareness, but not many people know why it's so important. Of course, it can allow a company to reach more viewers instantly and it gives customers a chance to engage with a brand directly, but there's a more science-based explanation for it, too.

Simply, visual content reaches an individual's brain in a faster and more understandable way than textual information. Or, more accurately, a person's brain is hardwired to recognize and make sense of visual information more efficiently, which is useful considering that 90 percent of all information that comes to the brain is visual.

If you consider body language, traffic signs, maps, facial cues, advertisements, and the plethora of other forms of visual communication a person experiences every day, it's not hard to see why our brains might have adapted to discern visual concepts more easily. For example, **40 percent of nerve fibers** in the brain are connected to the retina.

It also takes the brain longer to process text-based or verbal information, while the time it takes to process non-verbal, visual content is 0.25 seconds. Some sources even suggest that visuals are **processed 60,000 times faster than text**, which explains why we often find ourselves re-reading the same sentence eight times or staring at a page and realizing we have no idea what we've read.

It is believed that human communication has existed for over 30,000 years, but text-based communication has only been around for 3,700 years. So for the vast majority of human history, people have had to communicate without written word, meaning our brains had plenty of time to brush up on visual messages. Our brains became hard-wired to process visual data, including colors, which have been coded in our brains to represent certain messages or evoke specific emotions. **Exposure to the color red** increases pulse and breathing rates.

Measure the stopping power of your visuals with eyeQ Go.

Modern applications are already successfully experimenting with this information, with many mobile apps focusing on images, from Instagram and Snapchat to Pinterest and Vine. And it doesn't seem to be a passing trend: **Engagement per follower is 58 times higher** on Instagram than on Facebook.

According to the National Center for Biotechnology Information, the average customer's **attention span is eight seconds**, down from 12 seconds in 2000. That is officially less than the attention span of a goldfish (nine seconds). Our capacity to focus on one thing is diminishing, making the initial impression all the more valuable.

This is especially true for brick-and-mortar retailers launching an Omni-channel strategy: for shoppers with ever-increasing accessibility and ever-decreasing attention spans, their attention can be pulled in several different directions from in-store and digital to mobile and online; it's important to catch their attention quickly, but also through the right channel.

If it takes the human brain less than a second to interpret a single image or video, that leaves the brand more than seven seconds to engage with the customer how they see fit or, importantly, push the customer further down the path to purchase. And sharing visual content inside the store is easier than ever before **with digital technology**.

When combined with micro-location and customer insights, visual content gives retailers and brands the upper hand over competitors. It has been shown that website visitors spend 100 percent more time on pages with videos on them and, more impressively, shoppers are **85 percent more likely to purchase** an item after watching a product video.

Now go forth and share visually stimulating content.

https://www.eyeqinsights.com/power-visual-content-images-vs-text/

In my chapter on *Busted Tapping the Zone* images paid off for me big time. Both in my head and on paper. The situation was every time I needed a crew to assemble and secure our equipment they would send me different people. There was no time to sit down and read a book. So I created a picture book. I could take any individual and give them the book and they could see how each and every piece went on the pallet. Success, it worked every time no matter who they sent me.

It worked so well it was adopted by a higher command and was an essential part of my receiving an Air Force Medal.

I'm sure you have seen a picture of a new complex being developed in your city. It is key to getting projects approved and built.

Dyslexics may have a lack of words but we are very strong in the image or pictorial world.

CHAPTER 34

Present & Future Thinking vs Present & Past Thinking

This seems like it would be self-explanatory however, it's not that simple.

Imagine your thinking is only past and present and your decisions are based only on past results. Someone once said the definition of insanity is doing the same thing over and over again, expecting a different result.

Dyslexics typically think present and future. What are the possibilities? What if?

Many of our modern-day conveniences are a result of present and future thinking. Our cell phones are a perfect example. Because a dyslexic (Steve Jobs) asked, is it possible to touch a piece of glass and make it do something?

Henry Ford asked, what if we could mass produce an automobile and make it affordable to all?

CHAPTER 35

Believing vs Knowing

Imagination vs Facts

*You have to break a few eggs to make an omelet, okay? ~ **François de Charette**. No matter how many people question what you're doing, it's always part of a bigger plan. Just wait and see...*

You told them you were going to do this five hundred times. Why were they surprised when you actually did it?

This is an area that many Left-Brained (the majority) individuals have trouble understanding. As a Left-Brainer, you are inclined to make decisions based on the facts or what you know.

Dyslexics or Right-Brainers are inclined to make decisions on what they know plus what are the possibilities, you believe it will work. Many times a Right-Brainer will take what is known and maneuver, modify or adjust the situation to a better end. However, convincing a Left-Brainer that it's going to work can be a challenge. You can see the end result because of your visionary talents.

Warning: As Left-Brainers digest your idea, they many times will come to terms with the situation and concede that the idea will work. NOW it's presented as their idea! Ouch!

CHAPTER 36

Appreciates vs Acknowledges

Good leaders acknowledge, and Great leaders appreciate.

In my book *Leadership Leaves a Trail,* there are the seven C's of leadership.

Leadership is having the Courage to Clearly, Consistently and Compassionately Communicate a Commitment to a Community.

The word I'd like to focus on is Compassionately. Compassionately = Respect, Recognition, and Forgiveness.

- Respect = Appreciates.
- Recognition = Acknowledges.
- Forgiveness = Understanding the human factor. To error is human. We all do it!

A good leader will acknowledge your accomplishments. A great leader will appreciate your knowledge base, your history, and the value you bring to the table AND acknowledge your accomplishments.

These two items alone can make or break the human spirit.

Dyslexics are prone to leadership. So why is that? By the time a dyslexic individual reaches young adulthood, they have been pretty beaten up mentally.

As for myself getting out of high school was a blessing in that I was free of the stigma and could set my path.

I have reflected on my time in the military as having a sign on my forehead that said "Give it to Mikey he'll do it" As it turns out people see leadership in you. My mother called me an instigator. Call it karma, your aura, or as I was told "It is the way you carry yourself." "You have a strong presence."

If you don't like the path you are on, create your own.

CHAPTER 37

Spatial Perception vs Order/Pattern Perception

The spatial ability or visuospatial ability is the capacity to understand, reason, and remember the spatial relations among objects or spaces.

Visual-spatial abilities are used for everyday use from navigation, understanding or fixing equipment, understanding or estimating distance and measurement, and performing on a job. Spatial abilities are also important for success in fields such as sports, technical aptitude, **mathematics**, natural sciences, **engineering**, economic forecasting, **meteorology**, **chemistry**, and **physics**. Not only do spatial abilities involve understanding the outside world, but they also involve processing outside information and reasoning with it through visual representation in the mind.

Definition and types

Spatial ability is the capacity to understand, reason, and remember the spatial relations among objects or spaces. There are four common types of spatial abilities which include **spatial or visuo-spatial perception, spatial visualization, mental folding,** and **mental rotation**. Each of these abilities has unique properties and importance to many types of tasks whether in certain jobs or everyday life. For example, **spatial perception** is defined as the ability to perceive spatial relationships in respect to the orientation of one's body despite distracting information. **Mental rotation,** on the other hand, is the mental ability to manipulate and rotate 2D or 3D objects in space quickly and accurately. Lastly, **spatial visualization** is characterized as complicated multi-step manipulations of spatially presented information. These three abilities are mediated and supported by a fourth spatial cognitive factor known as **spatial working memory**. **Spatial working memory** is the ability to temporarily store a certain amount of visual-spatial memories under attentional control in order to complete a task. This cognitive ability mediates individual differences in the capacity for higher-level spatial abilities such as mental rotation. ~ Wikipedia

This has been of extreme value to me. When buying a house I can walk into a room and tell if the furniture is going to fit. When loading a vehicle or trailer I can see which boxes to load next for maximum use of space. When moving around the countryside it is difficult for me to get lost as I am always making mental notes of direction and terrain.

The most powerful gift to me is what is known as **Holographic Vision**. We can see things in 3D. We can rotate and see things from all angles, internally and externally.

When it comes to problem-solving we can take a situation, move, add/subtract information, and see a result. I commonly refer to this as the "What if Factor." This is common with DRBs yet difficult for a left-brainer to understand using only 2D visioning. You can see how this can be a big advantage in the engineering or architectural fields.

Order/Pattern Perception

This is an area where dyslexics are deficient. 9 P, 3 E, 6 9, can all look the same to a Dyslexic and take a long time to overcome. We never have trouble with 22, 55, 111, ee, or oo. A little dyslexic humor there. Given time and understanding, we will flourish.

CHAPTER 38

Adventurous vs Safe

Many dyslexics are very adventurous. This goes hand in hand with what are the possibilities. We are experiential learners with a high level of curiosity. If we can see the end result we don't get too worried about the details as we know those items will work themselves out. We are aware these details exist and in time the opportunity to take care of what is needed will present itself.

Because we can see the end result we are willing to take a higher risk. A higher calculated risk. I don't believe that dyslexics throw caution to the wind. However, to climbing a mountain there is always a risk factor.

On the other side, if we are always taking the safe route or being overly cautious, we don't learn and we don't grow as a person.

This can be frightening to a left-brained parent. If your whole world is practical and planned then someone who is impetuous and spontaneous seems to be radical and uncooperative. This causes a lot of friction between a dyslexic, right-brainer, and the majority of the world.

We are wired differently, therefore, we think differently. That's not a bad thing it is just a different thing.

EPILOGUE

For the Children

To all of the parents and educators of dyslexics, one must understand that dyslexia is the same as the color blue. The majority of the world is educated in the colors of red and green so when blue shows up in a child, the reds and greens are wondering what to do.

We all have left-brain and right-brain functions available to us. However, as we move through our education system and life all of us will tend to favor one side or the other. It is in the best interest of all of us to try and understand the differences in others.

It is my sincere hope that people will take the time to look past, what seems to be a disadvantage, and nurture the advantages that are just beneath the surface. Here are two important suggestions to parents of dyslexics that should be employed as early in their lives as possible:

Number One: work the hardest on keeping the dyslexic's self-esteem as high as possible. Focus on the things they get right and the things they like to do. That will give them more incentive to do the things they struggle with.

Number Two: If you can, find them positive support. Whatever it takes even if it means homeschooling. Many children in the school system are made fun of simply because they think differently. See differently as an advantage, not a disadvantage.

I saw an example of this from a psychologist.

Your child comes home with a report card that has an A, C, C, D, and an F. What would you do? Many will go straight to the F and try to fix it. Totally ignoring the better grades. At this point, the child is crushed. Feeling good about the good grades but there is no appreciation or acknowledgment of the better grades.

What's the cure? Psychologists know if you first emphasize and praise the good grades, keeping the individual's self-esteem high, then follow in a lower key underlining or being the help to improve the lower grades, the child will maintain good esteem and may aspire to bring the lower grades up.

Where would we be today without Dyslexics

Think about this... dyslexic's have brought us so many amenities that improve our lives.

The lights in our homes – *Thomas Edison*
The automobile – *Henry Ford*
The iPhone – *Steve Jobs*
Some of the best movies ever – *Stephen Spielberg*
Some of the best comedy ever – *Robin Williams*
HP Computers – *William Hewlett*
Language for computers – *Bill Gates*

Just to name a few.

About
Mike DeLong

Mike DeLong is a certified 100K Impact Coach and Certified with the American Union of NLP.

He is the founder of Mike DeLong International.

Mike believes that anyone can live an exceptional life. It's all about choices. It is choice - not chance that determines your destiny. He built a business starting from his basement to a multi-store retail operation, owns several businesses and has been in business for over 30 years. He is a decorated Airman and a master at tapping the zone.

He is no stranger to adversity. Born left-handed and Dyslexic he has had to meet the challenges of a seemingly difficult and backward world. He sees Dyslexia as a gift and is able to articulate that gift to others. Having a sister with a nero-muscular condition similar to Muscular Dystrophy and a brother that is mentally challenged he has grown up surrounded by challenged individuals which gives him a unique view of the word attitude. He has also done one of the hardest things a man can ever do (as stated by others). In 2007 he buried his son of 27 years. On his journey back to the normal world, Mike gained a much deeper and broader perspective on life.

Mike now dedicates his life to helping people understand their gifts and talents through Speaking, Workshops, Webinars, Teleconferences, and Coaching.

His mission is to use his education and experience to positively empower the lives of others.

To order copies of
The Gifts of Dyslexia,
please contact:

Mike DeLong
International, LLC

Mike@MikeDeLongInternational.com
♦ 303.249.4712 ♦
www.MikeDeLongInternational.com

Mike DeLong speaks at events, business
conferences, education and association
events.

Visit his website
www.MikeDeLongInternational.com
to learn more.